Life in the
THIRTEEN COLONIES

New York

Timothy J. Paulson

children's press®
An imprint of
■SCHOLASTIC

Library of Congress Cataloging-in-Publication Data

Paulson, Timothy J.
  New York / by Timothy J. Paulson.
    p. cm. — (Life in the thirteen colonies)
  Includes bibliographical references and index.
  ISBN 0-516-24575-9
  1. New York (State)—History—Colonial period, ca. 1600-1775—Juvenile literature. 2. New York (State)—History—1775-1865—Juvenile literature. I. Title. II. Series.
  F122.P38 2004
  974.7'102—dc22

                          2004007456

1 2 3 4 5 6 7 8 9 10 R 13 12 11 10 09 08 07 06 05 04

A Creative Media Applications Production
Design: Fabia Wargin Design
Production: Alan Barnett, Inc.
Editor: Matt Levine
Copy Editor: Laurie Lieb
Proofreader: Tania Bissell
Content Research: Lauren Thogersen
Photo Research: Annette Cyr
Content Consultant: David Silverman, Ph.D.

Photo Credits © 2004

Cover: Upper left © North Wind Archives; Upper right © North Wind Archives; Lower left © Getty Images/Hulton Archive; Lower right © North Wind Archives; Background © North Wind Archives; Title page © North Wind Archives; p. 2 © North Wind Archives; p. 4 © Corbis Bettmann/CORBIS; p. 7 © North Wind Archives; p. 12 © North Wind Archives; p. 19 © North Wind Archives; p. 22 © North Wind Archives; p. 25 © North Wind Archives; p. 27 © North Wind Archives; p. 30 © North Wind Archives; p. 33 © North Wind Archives; p. 37 © North Wind Archives; p. 40 © Tim Wright/CORBIS; p. 44 © North Wind Archives; p. 46 © North Wind Archives; p. 51 © North Wind Archives; p. 55 © Getty Images/Hulton Archive; p. 57 © North Wind Archives; p. 58 © North Wind Archives; p. 60: Top left © Getty Images/Hulton Archive; Top right © Colonial Williamsburg Foundation; Bottom left © Getty Images/Hulton Archive; Bottom right © Getty Images/Hulton Archive; p. 61: Top left © Getty Images/Hulton Archive; Top right © Getty Images/Hulton Archive; Bottom left © Colonial Williamsburg Foundation; Bottom right (jar) © Colonial Williamsburg Foundation; Bottom right (leech) © Anthony Bannister; Gallo Images/CORBIS; p. 62 © North Wind Archives; p. 66 © North Wind Archives; p. 71 © North Wind Archives; p. 70 © North Wind Archives; p. 74 © North Wind Archives; p. 77 © North Wind Archives; p. 81 © North Wind Archives; p. 81 © North Wind Archives; p. 86 © North Wind Archives; p. 88 © North Wind Archives; p. 95 © North Wind Archives; p. 97 © North Wind Archives; p. 98 © North Wind Archives; p. 101 © North Wind Archives; p. 104 © North Wind Archives; p. 109 © North Wind Archives; p. 110 © Joseph Sohm; Visions of America/CORBIS; p. 113 © North Wind Archives; p. 114 © North Wind Archives; p. 118 Upper left © North Wind Archives; Upper right © North Wind Archives; Lower left © Corbis Bettmann/CORBIS; p. 119: Upper left © Getty Images/Hulton Archive; Upper right © North Wind Archives; Lower left © North Wind Archives; Lower right © North Wind Archives; Background © North Wind Archives

CONTENTS

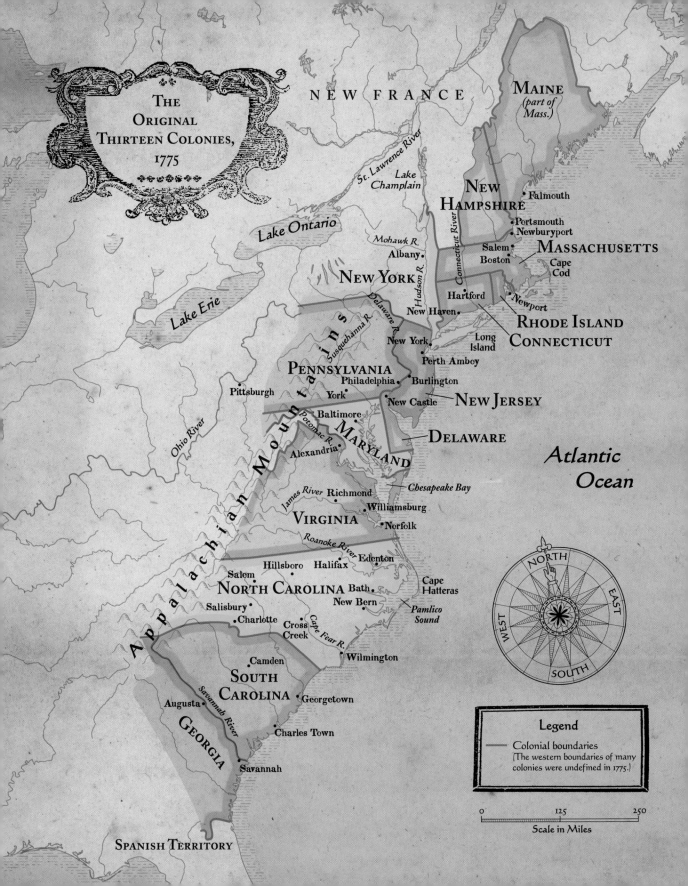

A Nation Grows
From Thirteen Colonies

New York lies in the northeastern region of the United States. It is bordered by Canada on the north, Vermont, Massachusetts, and Connecticut on the east, and New Jersey and Pennsylvania on the south. In the southeastern corner of the state, the island of Manhattan gives New York access to the Atlantic Ocean.

New York was home to the Algonquian people long before the first Europeans came to settle there. Beginning in the 1600s, Dutch and English settlers arrived and established towns and farms. These settlements grew to become the largest of the original thirteen colonies. New York City was the center of trade and business in the colonies. This is the story of how New York grew from a fur trading outpost into one of the most important parts of the young United States.

The map shows the thirteen English colonies in 1775. The colored sections show the areas that were settled at that time.

CHAPTER ONE

The Europeans Arrive

Henry Hudson

In Europe in the 1600s, the countries of China, India, and Japan were called the Far East. These countries were rich in spices, silk, tea, and other luxuries. Great demand for these goods in Europe made trade with the Far East very profitable for European sailors.

For a ship to reach the Far East at this time, it had to sail south from Europe all the way around the tip of Africa and then head east. The round-trip journey took more than a year and was very dangerous. In the open ocean, 40-foot (12-meter) waves could smash ships to pieces. If a shorter, safer water route from Europe to the Far East could be found, it would mean easier, quicker trips and greater wealth. A

❧ *In the 1600s, the journey to the Far East was very dangerous. Many ships were sunk by storms before reaching their destinations.*

trading company called the Dutch East India Company hired Captain Henry Hudson to find this shortcut.

Early in September 1609, while searching for the shortcut, Hudson sailed his ship, the *Half Moon,* into what is today New York Harbor. When Hudson saw the harbor, he believed his search was over.

The *Half Moon* had traveled thousands of miles across the Atlantic Ocean. Compared to oceangoing ships today, the 85-foot (26-meter) *Half Moon* (about the size of a city bus) would seem tiny. It had a crew of sixteen. Half of them were Dutch, and the other half were English. Like many ships of the time, the *Half Moon* was covered with brightly painted carvings. A red lion reared its head up over the back of the ship. Two huge lanterns hung on either side of it. A row of painted white diamonds dotted the ship's sides.

Henry Hudson made four voyages to the New World in small sailing ships like the Half Moon. *He was searching for a new route to the Far East.*

Trading for Food

One of the greatest challenges facing explorers in the sixteenth and seventeenth centuries was feeding the ship's crew on long ocean voyages. There were no refrigerators to keep food fresh. Even drinking water quickly became stale and infested with bugs after only a few days at sea. When ships encountered new lands and peoples, sailors were very eager to trade, especially for food and water.

This account from the logbook of the explorer Ferdinand Magellan in 1591 sums up what sailors of the time had to endure when no trade goods were available:

"We ate only old biscuit reduced to powder, and full of grubs, and stinking from the dirt which the rats had made on it when eating the good biscuit, and we drank water that was yellow and stinking. We also ate the ox hides which were under the main yard so that the yard should not break the rigging...also the sawdust of wood, and rats..."

Indians watched from the shore as Hudson's ship approached. One native story of the time described Hudson's ship as "a large house of various colors." The *Half Moon* was not the first European ship the natives had seen. European sea captains had been exploring the coast of North America for more than a hundred years when Hudson arrived in New York Harbor. But the Indians could not know that the arrival of the *Half Moon* would change their way of life forever.

Hudson Stakes a Claim

For months, Hudson had been sailing up and down the northeast coast of North America. He had poked into every large bay or inlet, hoping that it might be a water route that led across the continent to the Far East.

When he finally entered New York Harbor, Hudson thought he had found his shortcut. Before he sailed farther inland, he met with the Native Americans who lived on what would be called Manhattan Island. The Indians wanted to trade with the newcomers. As Hudson later said, the natives "flocked aboard the ship," offering apples, oysters, and beaver skins to trade. The sailors gave them knives and axes in return.

For weeks, Hudson and his men explored the harbor, traded with the natives, and got to know the area. Hudson was very impressed. As he later reported,

The land is the finest for cultivation I have ever in my life set foot upon.... It also abounds in trees of every description. The natives are a very good people; for, when they saw that I would not remain, they supposed that I was afraid of their bows, and taking the arrows, they broke them in pieces, and threw them in the fire.

Hudson headed up the waterway that he hoped would lead to the Far East. He sailed almost 150 miles (240 kilometers) inland (away from the coast). When he got to the rapids near what is today the city of Albany, he tasted the water. It was fresh, not salty like ocean water would be. Hudson realized that this waterway did not connect the two oceans. This was not the passage to the Far East. It was simply a very large river. With deep disappointment, he turned the *Half Moon* around and headed back to Europe.

Before he left, Hudson claimed all the lands touching this great river for the Dutch. He called the territory "New Netherland." The Netherlands was another name for the country also known as Holland, where the Dutch people lived. The great waterway Hudson had sailed up from New York Harbor would be named the Hudson River, in honor of the first European to sail upon it.

Life Before the Europeans

The first humans came to the New York region sometime between the years 1200 and 1400. In time, they divided into tribal groups. In the northern area of what would become New York, five separate tribes were established. They were called the Mohawk, Onondaga, Oneida, Cayuga, and Seneca. A group known as the Mahican settled near Albany. The Lenni-Lenape settled in lower New York and New Jersey.

The lives of the Indians were shaped by the dense forest that was their home. For food, they hunted deer, beavers, turkeys, rabbit, ducks, and black bears. They also fished for salmon and trout, which were plentiful in the rivers and streams of the area. Eventually, they cleared forest land and learned to farm. They grew mainly corn, beans, and squash. The natives called these crops "the Three Sisters." They also gathered nuts, berries, and roots from the forests. Wild herbs that grew in the woods were used for both food and medicine.

Woodland Indians kept themselves warm with clothes and blankets made from animal skins. They also made clothes from cornhusks. They decorated their bodies and their clothing with bones, feathers, and dyes made from berries and clay. Their spears and arrows were tipped with sharpened bone or turtle claws. Fish bones made fine fish-hooks. The natives also wove watertight baskets from reeds and built fish traps by weaving thin branches together.

The Three Sisters

The Native Americans planted corn, beans, and squash in a specific pattern called "the Three Sisters." This grouping, which was helpful to all three plants, showed how the woodland Indians understood their environment.

Beans grow on vine-like stems, which need to wrap themselves around poles. Cornstalks grow tall, providing perfect poles for the bean stems. Beans also make the soil richer as they grow. Squash grows low to the ground and produces large, flat leaves. These leaves protect the bases of all three plants, keeping weeds down and helping the soil to stay moist.

The Iroquois Nation

Before the arrival of the Europeans, the Indians of the northern New York region lived mostly in peace. The region was shared by the Mohawk, Onondaga, Oneida, Cayuga, and Seneca. They left each other's hunting and sacred sites alone.

As the Indian population grew, fights over land and hunting rights shattered the peace. Then, in the mid-1500s, a wise, powerful leader named Degandawidah came from the far north to this region. Degandawidah believed that if the native groups banded together, they would stop fighting each other. They could also better defend themselves against other tribes to the north and south. Indians from these areas were becoming serious rivals for the forests, fish, and game of the New York region.

Five Arrows

Before the current commemorative state quarters were issued, the U.S. twenty-five-cent piece had an eagle on the back. The eagle held five arrows in its talons. This image is a reminder of Degandawidah's message that strength comes from unity.

According to legend, Degandawidah gathered the leaders of the five tribes together. Standing before them, he held up a single arrow and broke it in two. He then bunched together five arrows and tried to break them, but together, they were too strong. The leaders all understood Degandawidah's point.

Hiawatha

Most people know the name of the great Indian leader Hiawatha from Henry Wadsworth Longfellow's famous poem *The Song of Hiawatha,* written in 1855. Wadsworth's poem was based on a sixteenth-century Native American, a chief of the Onondaga tribe.

Hiawatha was a powerful spiritual leader. He is believed to be the first Iroquois to have the idea of uniting the tribes.

Hiawatha set out to meet with the other Iroquois leaders. When he came to the Mohawk, he met with Degandawidah and told him of his ideas. After their meeting, Degandawidah went to the other tribes to convince them that they should unite.

Degandawidah used the five arrows to demonstrate the strength of Hiawatha's ideas. Both men were responsible for creating the Iroquois Nation.

Their people would be stronger as a group than they were as individual tribes. The chiefs agreed to unite into a single **alliance**. They called themselves "the people of the longhouse." Explorers and settlers knew them as the Iroquois. The name came from the French word for the common language that all these Indian tribes spoke. The tribes of the Iroquois alliance would control much of the fur trade in the New York region during the colonial period.

The Longhouse

The tribes of the Iroquois Nation shared the same language, and they also lived in the same style of home—the longhouse. Longhouses were built of timber and sod, with sloping roofs to shed rain and snow. Extended families lived together in one longhouse. Several longhouses clustered together formed a village. Women were in charge of each family, with the eldest woman making the main decisions. The village leader was usually, but not always, a man.

The Iroquois thought of their alliance as one great longhouse formed in the vast forests of New York. The Seneca

In addition to individual longhouses where people lived, many Iroquois villages had a larger longhouse that was used for ceremonies.

guarded the western door (the western section of the forest) and the Mohawk the eastern door (the eastern section). If invaders attacked from one side or the other, word would spread swiftly through the forest, and the attackers would be overwhelmed by warriors from many villages at once. Those who attacked one of the Iroquois tribes would have to face the united power of all the tribes together.

Lure of the New World

Europeans considered Europe the Old World. They called North and South America the New World, but it was new only to Europeans. Before Henry Hudson and other European explorers arrived, the native people had been living there for thousands of years.

By the time Hudson came to North America, the Lenni-Lenape had been trading with Europeans for about a hundred years. The natives were known as friendly and easy-going. They especially liked copper pots, steel tools, and other metal objects that the Europeans brought. The Indians could not make these things themselves. Similarly, the Europeans badly wanted the skins of otters and beavers that the Lenni-Lenape brought to trade. These animal skins were very valuable in Europe because they were used to make hats and expensive fur clothing.

Word Spreads

Upon Hudson's return home, stories of what he had discovered in the New World spread quickly through the Dutch capital city of Amsterdam. Amsterdam was one of the busiest ports in Europe. In its taverns and shops, other sailors and fur **trappers** returning from the New York region also told tales of what they had seen. They spoke of land that was good for farming. They reported that the Lenni-Lenape were friendly and open to trade. They explained that the harbor was deep and secure and that a mighty river led into the interior of the continent. Most important of all were the tales of beaver pelts and other animal furs.

Furs to Hats to Money

One way to understand how Dutch traders made their money is to look at hats. The most important fashion statement of the 1600s was a broad-brimmed, floppy hat. In almost every painting from that time that depicts wealthy Europeans, they are wearing these hats. The hat was more than a statement of taste. It was an extremely expensive status symbol. Its price at the time compared to that of a luxury car today. Owning one of these hats showed that a person was rich and important. The only way to make one of these hats was with the pelt of a beaver. As more people demanded luxury items like these hats, the prices went up, and the profits that could be gained from the fur trade increased.

Pelts are the skins of animals with the fur still on them. They were used to make hats and other clothes for wealthy Europeans. They were extremely valuable and very expensive. By the 1600s, most fur-bearing animals had been hunted almost to extinction in Europe. Trappers and traders had to travel far to find enough animal skins to meet the demand for them. News of the new source of furs around the Hudson River was very exciting. If Dutch trappers, traders, and settlers could go to America and bring back thousands of pelts, they could get rich.

The Dutch government formed a company to send people to North America to trade with the Indians for pelts. It was called the Dutch West India Company. But other countries also wanted a part of the rich fur trade in America. The Dutch therefore needed permanent settlers in America in order to protect their territory. So the Dutch West India Company offered settlers land and a chance for a better life in the New World in exchange for helping it set up a permanent colony there.

Soon, settlers and traders started making the journey across the Atlantic to the new Dutch colony. At this time, most of New York still belonged to the Indians of the Iroquois Nation. However, as the number of European settlers grew over the next several hundred years, the Indians would be forced to leave their lands and either adopt European ways or perish.

The River That Flows Both Ways

The Indians who lived in the area were called the Lenni-Lenape. The name means "original people." They had lived along the shores of the river that flowed north from New York Harbor for hundreds of years when Hudson arrived. They called the river Muhheakantuck, "the river that flows both ways." The Muhheakantuck's current flowed inland when the tide came in and toward the ocean when the tide went out.

European explorers were guided by maps such as this one from 1630. It shows New England and New Netherland, including New York Harbor and the Hudson River.

Europeans would rename the river in honor of Henry Hudson. Many Native American places were renamed by European explorers. Most Indian peoples did not have a system of writing. Their traditions and histories were passed by word of mouth from one generation to the next. As the natives were forced out of their lands, information about their tribes, including what they called the rivers, mountains, and forests, was often lost.

The Europeans made maps, kept journals, and had other written records. As more and more European explorers and settlers came to America, they gave new names to rivers, mountains, and other places. These names replaced the names that the Native people had used for centuries.

15

NEW FRANCE

NEW YORK, 1775

Lake Champlain

Saranac R.

St. Lawrence River

Oswegatchie R.

Adirondack Mountains

Fort Ticonderoga

NORTH

WEST EAST

SOUTH

Lake Ontario

Lake Oneida

Mohawk River

Saratoga

NEW YORK

Albany

MASSACHUSETT.

Lake Erie

Genesee River

Chemung River

Susquehanna R.

Catskill Mountains

Hudson River

CONNECTICUT

Appalachian Mountains

Delaware R.

PENNSYLVANIA

New York City (New Amsterdam)

Brooklyn

Long Island

Legend

Colonial boundaries
(The western boundaries of many
colonies were undefined in 1775.)

0   50   100

Scale in Miles

NEW JERSEY

Atlantic Ocean

MARYLAND

CHAPTER TWO

The Dutch Build a Colony

The First Dutch Colonists Arrive

In the late spring of 1624, a ship called the *New Netherland* set sail from Amsterdam. It carried thirty families on the month-long voyage to the New World. Most of these first colonists were married couples with skills in farming, trapping, or crafts such as carpentry, **blacksmithing**, and shoe-making. These skills would be very important for a permanent colony in the New World. The Dutch West India Company put Captain Cornelis May in charge of the group.

After more than two months at sea, the *New Netherland* landed in New York Harbor. The settlers and crew went ashore at the southern tip of Manhattan Island, where the Hudson River flows into the harbor. Captain May knew that this was an ideal spot for a settlement. As May and his group

☙ *This map shows how New York looked in 1775.*

of **colonists** came ashore, a few Dutch traders were already there to greet them. Small groups of fur traders had come to New Netherland soon after Henry Hudson first claimed the territory for Holland. A permanent trading post called Fort Orange had already been set up near present-day Albany, 150 miles (240 kilometers) up the Hudson River.

May wanted to establish Dutch settlements in as many places as possible, before other countries tried to claim the region. So he split up the settlers into four small groups. One group went up the Hudson River to Fort Orange. Another team went south to the Delaware River. A third went northeast to the Connecticut River. May and the remaining settlers built a small village on Manhattan Island. They named it New Amsterdam after Holland's chief city. This tiny, crude settlement would one day grow into the bustling modern metropolis known as New York City.

The settlers of New Amsterdam got along well with the Indians living in the region. They traded with the Lenni-

Lenape near Manhattan and with the Mahican and Mohawk near Fort Orange. "All as quiet as lambs" is how one woman described the Indians. With the help of the Lenni-Lenape, the settlers cut trees and planted crops. The Dutch knew good farmland when they saw it. One went so far as to say that,

The Dutch settlers who arrived in New Netherland in 1625 brought farming supplies and livestock, including cows and other animals.

except for a lack of pigs and cows, "whatever we desire in the paradise of Holland is here to be found."

In 1625, a ship from Holland sailed into the harbor with 103 head of livestock, farming tools, seeds, plants, guns, and items for trading with the Indians. The settlers were glad to receive the animals and supplies. Best of all, the ship brought new colonists, so there were now about 250 Dutch settlers in the colony. The new arrivals joined the original settlers in clearing land for farming. The ship also brought over a new colony director, Willem Verhulst. Then, with Captain May, 5,295 beaver pelts, and 463 otter skins from the New World aboard, the ship returned to Holland. The one-year-old colony was off to a good start.

A New Leader

Willem Verhulst remained in New Netherland for only a year. In 1626, another ship arrived from Holland with more colonists and another new leader named Peter Minuit. He had big plans for the new colony: he wanted ships from all over the world to come there to trade for furs and other goods.

A Fair Deal?

The value of the goods Peter Minuit traded to the Lenni-Lenape for Manhattan is often given as sixty guilders in Dutch money. This was equal to about $24 at the time and about $800 today. This seems like almost nothing for such a valuable piece of land. However, what today seems like an unfair deal probably did not appear unfair at the time.

The Indians who sold the island used the land to hunt and fish but did not live there. The Lenape probably did not see the items that Minuit gave them as a final payment for Manhattan. They expected to continue to hunt and fish on the island. They were really selling the Dutch the right to use the island along with the Indians.

On the other hand, the Dutch thought the island was theirs after the sale. In their eyes, the Indians had no further rights to Manhattan. This difference in the way each group viewed the trade would cause many problems as the colony grew.

First, Minuit needed to make sure that there would be no trouble with the Indians as the colony grew. He decided to buy the island of Manhattan from the Lenni-Lenape so the colony could expand. Minuit offered the Lenni-Lenape wool cloth, kettles, axes, hoes, drilling awls, and "diverse other wares." The Indians accepted the goods in return for the island.

Once Manhattan belonged to the Dutch, they had much work to do in order to create a true city. People were living in nothing more than dirt trenches with sod roofs. "Hovels and holes" is how one early colonist described them. These crude houses were cold, damp, and often filled with worms and insects. A permanent colony would need real wooden houses. More farmland had to be cleared and crops had to be planted. Most importantly, trade with the Indians, the major source of pelts, had to be strengthened. Trading had gone well so far, but there was trouble on the horizon.

Trouble With Trade

By the time Minuit arrived, trapping had nearly wiped out the beaver population near Manhattan. Fur traders had to trek almost 150 miles (240 kilometers) north to Fort Orange to trade for furs with the Mohawk and Mahican. The trip was long and dangerous. To make matters worse, these two Indian tribes were at war for control of the fur trade.

Before the arrival of the Dutch, the Mohawk and Mahican had lived in peace. In 1624, the two tribes began to fight over hunting grounds. They both wanted to trap as many beavers and other animals as possible to trade with the new settlers. They valued the metal pots, axes, cloth, and other goods they received in exchange for their furs. Each tribe wanted to drive the other away from the hunting grounds near Fort Orange.

The Dutch settlers in New Amsterdam made an agreement with the Mohawk to trade manufactured goods for furs.

The two tribes fought for four years to gain control of the region. Many Indians were killed or driven from their homes. Angry Indians from both sides attacked settlers and traders they thought were siding with their enemies. Dutch farms were raided, settlers were killed, and trade slowed to almost nothing. In 1628, the Mohawk finally drove the Mahican west, away from Fort Orange. Trade between the Mohawk and the Dutch then continued in peace, but the lives of both Indian tribes had been transformed by the new settlers.

The Mohawk-Mahican war also changed the settlers' lives. They became so afraid of attacks from Indians that they built a **stockade** around New Amsterdam. The settlers at the outposts on the Connecticut and Delaware rivers moved back to Manhattan. They wanted to be close to the fort in case of Indian attacks. When these colonists returned to New Amsterdam, there were more people to improve the town. Soon afterward, the settlers built a wind-powered **sawmill**, which they used to cut logs and planks. Then they built thirty wooden houses clustered around the fort.

Life in Early New Netherland

Even after these improvements, New Amsterdam was still a crude village. Unpaved streets became mud when it rained. In summer, horses and wagons raised great clouds of dust. The houses were made from rough boards. The roofs were made of dry thatch, or straw. Even the chimneys were wooden, which was very dangerous. Sparks from fireplaces often set houses on fire.

Most settlers lived on farms called *bouweries* surrounding New Amsterdam. For farmers, the day revolved around chores and working the land. Although the soil was rich, farming was not easy. Before crops could be planted, the land had to be cleared. Farmers picked up rocks from the fields and piled them into crude fences. Then they cut down trees and dug out the stumps. Teams of oxen hauled trees to the sawmill. There, logs were sliced into boards and beams to be used for houses and barns. The rest of the wood was chopped into firewood. Huge amounts of firewood were needed for cooking and warming the homes. The settlers

Work in New Netherland

The daily lives of the first New Amsterdam colonists were shaped by the tasks they had to perform. As the journalist and doctor Nicolaes van Wassenaer put it in a report published at the time,

"Men work there as in Holland. One trades, upwards, southwards and northwards; another builds houses, the third farms. Each farmer has his farmstead on the land purchased by the company, which also owns the cows; but the milk remains to the profit of the farmer; he sells it to those of the people who received their wages for work every week."

New Amsterdam was a small village in the early 1600s. But it had the basics for survival, including farms, a shipyard, a blacksmith's shop, and even a windmill.

grew or hunted everything they ate. Children milked the cows and gathered eggs from chickens.

The settlers made almost everything they needed themselves. Wheelwrights (wheel makers) and carpenters built wagons for carting. Blacksmiths made metal tools and a constant supply of nails. When tools got dull or damaged, they had to be reworked. When metal tools wore out, the metal was reused to make new tools.

wanted to own their own land and their own businesses. They did not want to travel all the way to America just to work for the Dutch West India Company.

As a result, New Netherland grew much more slowly than the English colonies of Massachusetts and Virginia. By 1640, there were only about 500 settlers in the entire colony. In contrast, the English colonies each had thousands of permanent residents by this time. The population of New Netherland would grow in time, but first the colony would go through three new leaders and fight a war over pigs.

Women to the Rescue

The women of the Dutch households were very hardworking. Even in the early days of New Amsterdam, they kept the insides of their homes very clean. They scrubbed the floors daily and washed clothes by hand. These chores fascinated Indian women who visited the settlement. They did not understand why Dutch women kept the insides of their houses so clean while they often piled garbage outside and allowed pigs, cows, and chickens to roam in the yard. Indian women spent much less time housecleaning, but they kept their homes orderly and neat inside and out.

Rensselaerswyck

Almost all the settlers in New Netherland lived in or near New Amsterdam. Farms slowly spread north on Manhattan, onto Long Island, and up the Hudson River. Most of these farms and settlements were within a few days' travel from New Amsterdam. This made it possible for the farmers to get supplies and sell goods in the city.

A few hardy settlers established farms near Fort Orange. These frontier settlements were far away from the supplies and safety of New Amsterdam. Frontier settlers lived very difficult lives. They had to make, grow, hunt, or trade for everything they ate or used. They were constantly in danger of Indian attacks and had to live through long, cold winters. Few colonists were willing to live this very hard life. Those who did were more often trappers than farmers.

One Dutch family, the van Rensselaers, was granted more than 330,000 acres (132,000 hectares) near Fort Orange in 1629. The van Rensselaers received this huge tract of land, called Rensselaerswyck, in exchange for bringing fifty new settlers to New Netherland. The new settlers worked for the van Rensselaers. Although the Dutch government offered other wealthy Dutch citizens similar land grants if they brought settlers to New Netherland, the idea never caught on.

The main business of the settlers in Rensselaerswyck was trading with the Mohawk and other Indian tribes for beaver pelts.

CHAPTER THREE

New Netherland Grows Up

Two New Governors

The Dutch West India Company sent a new director named Wouter van Twiller to expand the colony in 1633. Unfortunately, van Twiller was much more interested in buying land for himself and his friends than attracting new colonists. He let New Amsterdam fall into disrepair. After four years, the company fired him in 1637 and sent another director named Willem Kieft to take his place.

When Kieft came ashore in 1638, the colony was in terrible shape. He reported back to the company directors in Holland, "The fort is open at every side; except the stone point; the guns are dismounted; the houses and public buildings are all out of repair." Indeed, the buildings were falling

☙ *When Governor Kieft arrived in New Amsterdam, he immediately started planning ways to improve the colony.*

31

apart. The company farms on Manhattan Island were overgrown. Many of the original thirty houses built by the first settlers were now occupied by hogs and chickens. The company storehouse had burned down and only two mills still worked. Jails were filled with men who had been arrested for fighting, assault, and murder. Most of these crimes were the result of excessive drinking. Also, the local officials did not enforce the laws. They allowed people to do pretty much as they wished.

Kieft cracked down with an iron hand. He made liquor sales illegal anywhere but in the company store. He passed a number of laws to cut down on crime. Any colonist who sold guns or gunpowder to Indians could be hanged. Kieft **imposed** a nine o'clock curfew, which meant that all townspeople had to be in their homes by that hour at night or face arrest. He also ordered company workers to put in a full day's work every day and to take their responsibilities to the company more seriously. Many settlers disliked him immediately because he was so strict.

In addition to new rules and laws, Kieft began to make improvements in the town. The fort was fixed up, a church was built, and a fine stone house was built for the director himself. Kieft also ordered the building of two new roads, in order to connect the town to areas containing open farmland. One road led to the north end of Manhattan Island. The other led to a ferryboat that crossed the strait on the east side of the island to Long Island, which was part of the colony. These roads made travel and trade with farms in both places much easier.

Even though Kieft was disliked, he got things done, and the colony started to prosper and grow again. New settlers arrived from Holland. In addition, a group of Puritans from Massachusetts moved to Long Island. The Puritans were a religious group that had settled in the Massachusetts Bay Colony. Some Puritans became dissatisfied with the Massachusetts government and left to establish farms and communities elsewhere. They liked the idea that the Dutch accepted people of all religions.

Governor Kieft organized the people of New Amsterdam and made many improvements to the town. He built new roads and fixed up the houses and wind-powered sawmill.

The Pig War

After a year of getting things in order, Kieft made a terrible mistake in 1639. He demanded that the Lenape and other Indian tribes in the region pay taxes to the company. These taxes were supposed to pay for protection provided by the Dutch against attacks by the Mohawk. The Lenape were furious.

From their point of view, the Europeans had come to their shores without an invitation. The Lenape had given the newcomers food and helped them survive when they first arrived. They had never been repaid for this help. At no time had the Dutch done anything to protect the Lenape or other tribes living near Manhattan. The Indians refused to pay the taxes.

Kieft's attempts to make them pay turned the Indians against the Dutch settlers. The situation grew worse and worse over the next two years. Kieft organized raids on Indian villages to show his power over them. The Indians fought back and began to attack Dutch settlements and farms.

Then, in 1641, a Dutch farmer on Long Island accused a group of Indians of stealing his pigs. Kieft overreacted to the incident. He sent eighty soldiers to punish the Indians. In the violent fight that followed, at least four Indians and four Dutch settlers were killed. The Pig War had begun.

Massacre

Fights between the Indians and Dutch continued on and off for another two years. Then, in the summer of 1643, an Indian killed a colonist in present-day New Jersey. When the natives who lived there refused to give up the killer, Kieft saw his chance to get revenge on the Indians. He sent his soldiers across the Hudson River to kill them.

A Dutch settler described the slaughter. He wrote of soldiers returning from the raid who boasted of Indian babies "torn from their mother's breasts, and hacked to pieces in the presence of their parents." The colony's soldiers killed dozens of Native American men, women, and children.

The Indians took their revenge. They burned settlers' farms and killed whole families. Dutch farmers raced to the fort in New Amsterdam for protection, and trade between the Indians and the colonists came to a standstill. When the fighting finally

The Truth About the Pigs

The pigs that started the Pig War were actually stolen by sailors working for the Dutch West India Company. The sailors blamed the theft on the local Indian tribe, and their Dutch bosses and the farmer who owned the pigs believed the accusation. The stolen pigs were just the excuse Kieft needed to attack the Indians and try to make them pay taxes.

ended in 1645, more than 500 Indians had died at the hands of Kieft's troops.

The company did not like anything that hurt profits and risked the future of New Netherland. Kieft had violated the company motto, "'Tis better to rule by love and friendship than by force." The company ordered Kieft to return to Holland. Many of the improvements he had overseen in the colony were wiped out by four years of bloody fighting.

The General Arrives

The Dutch West India Company feared that its colony had been ruined. The company knew that it had to select someone with the right combination of strength and courage to take over New Netherland. It chose Peter Stuyvesant.

Stuyvesant was a crusty veteran soldier. His leg had been shot off by a cannonball when he was fighting for the company in the Caribbean. He now wore a wooden leg studded with silver nails. The General, as he liked to be called, was known for his stubbornness and intelligence. He was also known to be extremely intolerant of anyone who was different from him. Stuyvesant hated Jews, blacks, and Catholics. In fact, he disliked anyone who did not belong to the Dutch Reformed Church. Many New Netherland colonists had gotten used to being around people of different backgrounds, and they did not like his intolerant attitude. They called Stuyvesant many nicknames behind his back. "Stubborn Pete" was probably the nicest.

When Stuyvesant arrived in New Netherland in 1647, he found the colony in a shambles. He noted that the "land-destroying and people-expelling wars" that Kieft had started had emptied the colony of its best people. The streets were filled with garbage. Fences were falling down and pigs, chickens, cows, and geese roamed everywhere. The town's 700 or so people were crammed into 120 dilapidated houses. Stuyvesant decided to take drastic action to save the colony.

Peter Stuyvesant was sometimes called "Pegleg Pete" because he had a wooden leg.

A New Order

Stuyvesant's first aim was to bring order to the colony. "I shall rule you as a father his children," he declared. Then he quickly set up new rules for everyone. Throwing garbage into the streets was outlawed. Animals were no longer allowed to run free through the town. Women could be fined for raising their skirts to cross a muddy street. Stuyvesant thought this was "indecent."

For breaking the law, citizens were either fined or placed in wooden stocks as punishment. The stocks were a device that held a person's head, hands, and feet so he or she could not move. It was placed in the middle of town so everyone could see the offender. Anyone in the stocks would be made fun of by passersby and even hit or kicked.

Stuyvesant created the colony's first police force, called the "rattle watch." From the time the taverns closed at night until the sun came up the following morning, nine watchmen in orange and blue coats walked the streets, carrying swords, pistols, and rattles. If a watchman spotted

School Life in New Netherland

The Dutch believed in plenty of schooling and strong discipline. The typical school day was six hours, and the school year ran for 250 days. The standard school year today is only 180 days. Arithmetic, writing, and reading were the main subjects. In addition, all students participated in prayer and religion classes. Boys sat at the front of the class, and girls sat at the back. Children who misbehaved received sharp blows from rods made of willow branches or were made to sit on tacks or hold heavy books on their heads.

trouble, he shook his rattle to make a loud noise and attract help from the other watchmen.

Stuyvesant also arranged for many other public services. Since fire was a danger because many chimneys were still made of wood, he organized fire crews. Leather fire buckets were placed throughout the town. When a building caught on fire, everyone formed lines to pass buckets of water to put out the blaze. However, a person whose house caught fire was fined for being careless.

Order in New Netherland

Stuyvesant had the streets paved with **cobblestones**. This made them safe for travel. He also had the fort repaired. The rundown windmills were rebuilt to grind grain and saw timber. A wall was added at Wall Street for protection from Indian attacks.

Stuyvesant saw the lack of schools and teachers as a major problem. The company had long promised to improve education in the colony. It had built a schoolhouse and brought over a few teachers as early as 1628, but Stuyvesant brought in many more teachers and provided money to run the schools.

Additional Dutch troops also came to provide security for the colonists. Soon, new villages appeared throughout the Dutch territory. The town of New Amsterdam became a much more civilized place to live, but this did not make everyone happy. Stuyvesant paid for the improvements by taxing the citizens. Colonists had to pay taxes on liquor and on any furs they sold. This made Stuyvesant very unpopular with the people, but the strong-willed leader did not seem to mind. He had accomplished his goal. He had restored order in New Netherland.

A Very Dutch Diversity

Stuyvesant's changes made New Netherland so attractive to new settlers that people from many countries poured into the colony. In 1654, the first Jews arrived in New Amsterdam. Free black people (those who were not slaves) from Angola and other parts of Africa joined those who had already made their way into New Amsterdam society. Citizens of nearly every country in Europe came to New Netherland.

Stuyvesant was not pleased with all the new people. He objected to the wide range of cultures that thrived in his colony. He even wrote a nasty letter to the company asking that "none of the Jewish nation be permitted to infest New Netherland." The company responded firmly, insisting that Stuyvesant had to allow people of all backgrounds into the colony.

In 1657, a group of Quakers came to New Amsterdam seeking religious freedom. The Quakers, also known as the Society of Friends, were an English religious group that did not believe in the authority of priests. Their beliefs caused them to be persecuted in England. Many Quakers came to America to start a new life. They first settled in the Massachusetts Bay Colony, but soon found life under the strict Puritan rules of Massachusetts little better than it had been in England. Long Island had plenty of farmland and the Dutch had a reputation for religious tolerance.

Quakers sometimes preached in the streets of New Amsterdam even though Stuyvesant made it illegal for them to practice their religion in public.

There was only one problem. Stuyvesant hated Quakers as much as he hated Jews. He allowed both groups in his colony only because the company forced him to do so. Stuyvesant did not allow either group to build churches or synagogues. They could worship freely—as long as they did it in their homes and not in public.

Africans in New Netherland

Slaves and free blacks had always been a part of New Amsterdam. The first free blacks came to New Netherland with Dutch traders around 1613. They were crew members on Dutch ships. The first slaves arrived in 1626, on board a ship owned by the Dutch West India Company. These eleven slaves built houses, roads, and bridges. They planted and harvested crops. Then more and more slaves arrived, making the Dutch the leaders in the slave trade.

Throughout the 1600s, Dutch ships carried thousands of slaves from Africa to the New World. Dutch merchants made enormous amounts of money from buying and selling slaves. Even so, most Dutch citizens did not like the idea of owning people. As a result, the Dutch West India Company came up with the idea of half-slavery. This gave slaves some rights, but they remained slaves.

In half-slavery, the master owned the slave's labor, but not his or her personal life. Therefore, many Dutch slaves lived away from their masters' houses in their own homes. They were allowed to earn small amounts of money by working for others, and their masters sometimes gave them money to pay rent and buy food.

Masters were not allowed to whip or severely punish slaves without permission from the court. Slaves were not required to carry passes when they were away from their masters' property, as was the case in other colonies. They also had the right to gather in groups and they could own property. Slaves were allowed to marry, and husbands could protect their wives from cruel masters. Slaves could even sue their masters in court and testify against white people. Slaves in the other colonies had none of these rights.

Even though Dutch slaves received better treatment than slaves in other colonies, especially in the South, they were still not free. In New Amsterdam, Peter Stuyvesant used slaves to build roads and tend the company farms. This made economic sense for the company. In 1646, the average yearly wage for a laborer was 600 guilders (Guilders are Dutch money). A slave cost about 300 guilders plus his or her upkeep. That made slave labor very economical for Stuyvesant and the company.

Many Dutch slaves in New Amsterdam worked alongside their masters as skilled tradesmen. By 1664, there were about 8,000 whites living in the city and about 700 slaves. In addition, many free blacks lived and worked in New Amsterdam. Escaped slaves from other colonies came to New Amsterdam to hide. Because there were many free blacks in the city, they could blend in. Also, there were jobs available to free black people, so they could support themselves and their families.

How Much Is That Worth?

The value of money has changed a great deal in the past 400 years. It is difficult to compare what something was worth in the mid-1600s with what it would be worth today. One way is to compare "buying power"—how many goods and services a given amount of money can buy. In 1640, 600 guilders would buy about the same amount of food, clothing, housing, and other goods and services as $7,300 today.

Two Threats

In 1655, a group of Swedish settlers established a settlement in Dutch territory. "Pegleg Pete," as Stuyvesant was sometimes called, was furious. Intending to throw them out of his colony, Stuyvesant led 600 soldiers on seven ships from New Amsterdam south to Delaware and the Swedish colony. The Swedes gave up almost immediately and fled the colony.

When Stuyvesant returned to New Amsterdam a few weeks later, he was shocked to find the colonists in a violent conflict with Native Americans. The cause of the violence was the tragic killing of a young Indian girl who had gone

In 1655, Indians attacked Dutch farms and the settlers raided Indian villages.

into an orchard to pick a peach. The Dutch farmer who owned the orchard had shot the girl to death. Several Indian tribes struck back, invading the city and destroying homes, raiding farms and killing settlers. The fighting spread quickly. When it was over, twenty-eight farms had been destroyed. Fifty settlers were killed and others were captured. Sixty Indians died in the fighting, as well.

Many colonists called for Stuyvesant to attack the Indians, but he refused. Stuyvesant believed that the colonists were at fault for killing the Indian girl for such a small crime as taking a peach. He remembered how Kieft had almost ruined the colony by fighting with the Indians in the Pig War. So, instead of attacking, Stuyvesant negotiated with the Indians. All prisoners were released, and tempers on both sides finally calmed down. Stuyvesant's stubbornness and diplomacy paid off for everyone involved. As a result, both sides lived in peace for the remainder of Stuyvesant's time as governor.

A Shift in Power

Despite these successes, Stuyvesant's harsh rule and intolerant attitude toward those who were different from him made many colonists dislike the governor. In addition, although he improved conditions in the colony, he also imposed heavy taxes on the settlers. Many considered him a tyrant. Over time, the colonists convinced the Dutch authorities to allow them a greater say in the colony's government and to limit Stuyvesant's powers. They formed a new town council that gave some of New Amsterdam's citizens the chance to help run the city.

In the end, the colonists would show their unhappiness with Stuyvesant by refusing to fight for New Netherland against an outside invader. As a result, the Dutch would lose control of the colony they had struggled so hard to build.

CHAPTER FOUR

The English Seize New Netherland

Life in New Netherland

By the mid-1600s, Dutch settlers had lived in the colony of New Netherland and the city of New Amsterdam for about forty years. Their colony was a great success. The colonists were trading for valuable furs with the Indians. Ships sailed in and out of New Amsterdam Harbor, carrying goods back and forth from Holland. Settlers were growing crops and harvesting lumber from the forests. New settlements now spread out on the island of Manhattan as farmers cleared more land. New Amsterdam was becoming one of the most important cities in America. Stuyvesant's strict leadership had made his colony into a great success. All of that was about to change.

By the mid-1600s, New Amsterdam was a thriving community. The harbor was filled with ships from all over the world that came there to trade.

York Harbor. With the aid of Dutch farmers who were angry over their treatment by the British, Evertsen captured the city with little fighting. The Dutch changed the city's name to New Orange, for Holland's Prince of Orange. The New York colony was New Netherland once again.

Dutch rule was not to last. Holland was getting tired of its war with England and could not afford to fight anymore. A year after Evertsen took the colony, Holland handed it back to the English.

The Duke's Laws

When the English took over New York, they imposed their laws. They were called the Duke's Laws because the colony was ruled by the Duke of York. The Duke's Laws set up a court system to enforce the laws that governed people's everyday lives.

The laws affected Indians as well as the English and Dutch. They could not follow their religion. The law said, "No Indian whatsoever shall at any time be suffered to powaw [powwow] or perform outward worship to the Devil in any Towne within this Government."

The English thought of the Indian's religion as devil worship and wanted it stopped.

Each town had to have a church that held at least 200 people. Preachers were required to preach every Sunday and pray for the royal family.

The laws made killing wolves profitable. They stated that anyone "who kills a wolf would receive a payment by bringing the head to a constable [sheriff]." The payment would be "to the value of an Indean [Indian] coat."

The British Return

Now that he had control of New York again, the Duke of York sent a young army officer named Edmund Andros to govern the colony. Andros made dramatic improvements to the town. Stuyvesant's old canal near the waterfront had become polluted. The new governor ordered it filled in and paved and built a new covered market on the same site. Great stone piers were built as the foundations for new waterfront forts. New wells were also dug to bring fresh water to the city.

A Change of Leadership

In 1683, Andros was replaced as governor of New York by Colonel Thomas Dongan. At this time, the colonists were calling for a greater voice in their government. Dongan gave it to them in the form of the General Assembly. Members of the assembly would be elected by the colonists to make laws for the colony. Only men who owned land and wealthy tradesmen and merchants could vote for the assembly.

The first set of laws passed by the assembly was called the Charter of Liberties and Privileges, signed in 1683. These laws included the right to free speech, trial by jury, and the right of the colonists to have a say in how they would be taxed. The town proclaimed the charter's passage with a trumpet blast and sent it off to the Duke of York for his approval. When the duke approved the charter, everyone was pleased. The rich were happy with the power they had in the assembly and the poor at least had some of their rights spelled out in writing.

A Time of Change

In 1685, word came from England that King Charles II had died. His brother, James, the Duke of York, was the new king of England. At first, the New York colonists thought this was great news. The duke had approved the Charter of Liberties and Privileges. Surely, he would give them even more freedom now that he was king.

But King James II, as he was now called, had other ideas for his colonies in the New World. First, he sent the former governor, Edmund Andros, back to America. This time, the king made Andros more than just the governor of New York. He became governor of the Dominion of New England, which included the colonies of New York, Connecticut, Massachusetts, New Hampshire, New Jersey, Rhode Island, and Plymouth (which later became part of Massachusetts). James thought that placing all the English colonies in the region under the leadership of one governor would make them easier to rule. Andros immediately raised taxes and took away the charters of all the individual colonies. Colonists in New York and the other English colonies were extremely unhappy with these events.

As it turned out, the new government did not last long. Word arrived in 1688 that James II was no longer king. He had been replaced on the throne by his daughter, Mary, and her husband, William. Angry colonists seized this opportunity to imprison Andros and send him back to England. His

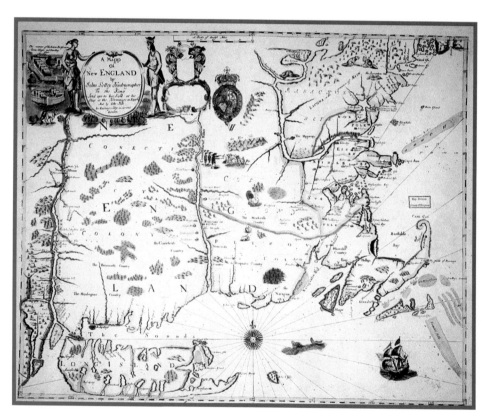

This map of New England from 1675 shows the territory that King James II wanted to combine into one large colony.

ship sank in a storm before he reached home. The Dominion of New England died with Andros and the colonies returned to their individual governments. The new king and queen appointed Francis Nicholson as governor of New York.

Leisler's Rebellion

New York's colonists did not trust the new governor or the "government of tyrants" in England that he represented. Rumors spread through the colony that French settlers from New France and their Native American allies were going to attack Fort Orange, which the British had renamed Albany. The French controlled most of what is now Canada, including the territory west of New York.

The colonists feared that the English would not protect them. Angry mobs filled the streets of New York City. Grabbing rakes, hoes, and whatever else they could find to use as weapons, they marched to the fort in New York Harbor. The mob quickly overpowered the few British soldiers stationed there and took control of the city. The colonists then voted for a new leader. His name was Jacob Leisler.

Jacob Leisler's followers overwhelmed the British soldiers who guarded the fort in New York Harbor.

Leisler held elections in which tradesmen became police officers and judges. For the first time, he allowed many poorer New Yorkers to vote. He also **repealed** some laws that treated ordinary people unjustly. This made the common people very happy, but rich New Yorkers hated and feared him.

While Leisler was making far-reaching changes in New York, Nicholson decided to return home to England.

He accused Leisler and his followers of seizing the government illegally and convinced the king and queen that they had to take back the colony by force. William and Mary appointed a new governor named Henry Sloughter and sent English troops to take New York from Leisler.

When the English troops landed in the city, they were met by Leisler's **militia**. Leisler ordered his men to shoot. Two English soldiers were killed and several more soldiers were wounded. Leisler's militia was greatly outnumbered. He was arrested, tried, and found guilty of treason. On May 16, 1691, Leisler was hanged.

Leisler's influence did not die with him, however. Many of the unjust laws he repealed were never reinstated. In 1695, some of his followers were elected to the General Assembly. From this point forward, thanks to Leisler, the people of New York realized that they could have a say in their government.

Slaves and Free Blacks

New York's slaves and free black residents did not prosper under English rule. Many free black city residents had owned property under Dutch rule. They were barred from this right by a new law passed in 1712.

When they took over New York, the English immediately did away with half-slavery. They strengthened the rights of slave owners and granted them life and death power over their slaves. In addition, the English encouraged slave trading because of the great profits it brought to the colony.

New York became the slave trading capital of the northern colonies. By 1747, one-fifth of the people in New York City were slaves. The Royal African Company established a slave market on Wall Street. It was a "place where Negroes and Indians could be bought, sold, or hired," according to newspaper reports and advertisements from the time.

The lives of slaves in New York were not as difficult as in most southern colonies, but slaves had very few rights under English rule. Slaves had to have passes when they were away from their masters' property, and no more than four blacks (free or slave) could meet together at once. While cruel treatment such as whipping was discouraged by the English government, it was not outlawed. Slaves lived in poverty, and most longed for their freedom.

Slaves were bought and sold at New York's waterfront slave market.

Colonists could consult a medical professional, such as a physician, a surgeon, or an apothecary. But they often used home remedies to cure themselves. These medicines were made from herbs and other things gathered from the environment.

☞ *The fear of being shot was a constant worry. So doctors carried bullet extractors in their medical kits.*

♤ *Medical records were kept in journals.*

🖐 *Some surgical tools looked more like weapons than modern medical instruments. This large knife was used to cut off limbs.*

🖐 *Many colonial doctors traveled through the countryside to treat sick people on farms and in small towns. They carried everything they needed in chests like this one.*

✍ A small cut was made in the patient's skin with this lancet to allow the "bad blood" to flow out.

⚖ Surgical scissors have not changed much since colonial times.

🎺 The village apothecary measured and weighed the ingredients for each medication.

☞ No apothecary shop was complete without a supply of leeches. Leeches were placed on the skin to bleed the patient. This process was thought to rid the body of the cause of sickness.

LEECHES

CHAPTER FIVE

A New City for a New Century

Making New York English

As the years went by, more and more English-style buildings were built in New York City. By 1698, work was completed on Trinity Church. This was the first house of worship in the city built in the English style, with a tall, sharp spire. A few years later, a new town hall was built to replace the rundown state house that had been put up by Peter Stuyvesant. Even the old city wall, built by Stuyvesant on what is today Wall Street, was knocked down for good.

By 1700, the population of the New York colony had grown to 20,000. This was almost double what it had been when the English had taken over thirty-six years before. Most of New York's colonists were still Dutch. They still

New York's docks were an important part of the city. Sailors from all over the world met here to exchange stories and sign up for duty on a new ship.

100 pounds a year or more for those shopkeepers who could afford it. One hundred pounds would be about $6,000 today.

Money poured into New York from trade with the other colonies and with Europe. Soon, simple tradespeople discovered that they could afford to buy their own homes and shops. New construction created more jobs for bricklayers, carters (people who haul things), stonecutters, and carpenters. As these workers made more money, they built homes of their own. The businesses of the shopkeepers and merchants who furnished those homes also grew. People of all classes benefited from the city's growth.

One of the ways the various classes in New York told themselves apart was through their clothing. The wealthy were known to working people as "bigwigs" and "silk stockings." Their fancy clothes and elaborate hairdos advertised their high status in the community. The poorest New Yorkers showed their positions through their rough, patched clothes.

Bigwigs

Most wealthy residents of New York wore wigs. The richest male citizens showed their importance by wearing extremely large wigs. In 1690, only fifty of New York City's 5,000 people wore the big wig. They all had to pay a special tax for the privilege. Naturally, New Yorkers began to call these people "bigwigs." Today, the term means any important person.

Wealthy New York merchants conducted business from offices such as this one.

Food and Entertainment

The rich often entertained at home, hosting card parties and masked costume balls. The food was usually very fancy. As such social events became more important, rich New Yorkers bought carriages to ride through the city streets. The clothes they wore to attend parties became fancier. Manners, like everything else in New York, became more like those in London, England's capital.

Food and entertainment among the poor changed little during this time. Oysters were the most common of all New York foods. The poor often ate little else except oysters and bread. For a living, they gathered oysters from the marshes surrounding the city and sold them on the streets. Henry Hudson had traded for oysters with the Lenni-Lenape a hundred years earlier. The first Dutch settlers had used oysters mainly to feed their pigs. Poor colonists now ate so many oysters that the crushed shells were used as building material for Manhattan's Pearl Street. Variety in the diet was enjoyed mainly by the middling and richer classes.

An innkeeper named Samuel Fraunces opened the first of his several taverns on upper Broadway in the mid-1700s. Later, he would shift its location to an unoccupied mansion further downtown, near the city's

Bowling on the Green

In 1732, the town council opened a park known as the Bowling Green on the southern tip of Manhattan Island. The Dutch had been playing a game called ninepins there for nearly a century. When a law was passed against playing ninepins on Sundays, the Dutch simply added a tenth pin, making the game into the modern sport of bowling, and kept on playing.

poorhouse. Fraunces's Tavern would be celebrated for decades as one of New York City's finest establishments. George Washington would say good-bye to his troops at Fraunces's Tavern in 1783, after the Revolutionary War.

By the mid-1700s, the social structure of New York was firmly in place. For the most part, the city was thriving. However, dark clouds were gathering in New York and throughout all thirteen British colonies in America. Political events would soon sweep New York into a great war.

CHAPTER SIX

The Seeds of Revolution

Fighting for a Continent

By the mid-1700s, New York was one of thirteen English colonies in North America. However, England was not the only European country to own colonies on the continent. France had also established a colony called New France in what is now Canada. Both nations wanted to control the rich trade and natural resources of America. They were willing to go to war to achieve that goal.

From the end of the 1600s to the middle of the 1700s, France and England fought a series of wars to take control of the North American continent. The first three wars between the French, the English, and their Indian allies were called King William's War (1689–1697), Queen Anne's War

🖎 *Young George Washington read prayers to his troops and Indian allies before going into battle in the French and Indian War.*

(1701–1713), and King George's War (1744–1748). All had pretty much the same result. Although soldiers and natives battled up and down the continent, from snowbound frontier settlements in New York to the steaming swamps of Florida, neither side won. It would take a larger war than the continent had ever seen to bring this struggle to an end.

The French and Indian War

In the summer of 1754, twenty-two-year-old Lieutenant George Washington led a group of Virginia soldiers into the wilderness of western Pennsylvania. Washington's troops were fighting for the British. His objective was to attack the French, who had built a fort in the Ohio Valley. Washington hoped to drive the French from the area. A victory would give England control of the fur trade throughout the region.

Washington's raid failed. Indian warriors and French soldiers dressed as Indians were waiting for him. They appeared from out of nowhere, firing from behind rocks and trees. As casualties piled up and no help arrived, Washington was forced to surrender. The French sent Washington and the remainder of his troops back to Virginia. With this small but fierce fight, the French and Indian War began.

It would not be long before this war came to the New York colony. With the border of New France only 300 miles (480 kilometers) north of Manhattan, New York City was prepared for attacks throughout the nine years that the war dragged on. The war never came to New York City, but people in northern New York felt its fury.

Farmers and settlers in northern New York were constantly raided by Indians loyal to the French. Both British and French troops and their native allies suffered from starvation and disease. The troops were often short of supplies, including food. There were even reports of cannibalism on both sides during the long, cold winters.

The first years of the French and Indian War went badly for the British. But by 1757, their luck began to change. The British captured two forts on Lake Champlain in northern New York, giving them control of this important waterway.

British troops captured Fort Ticonderoga on Lake Champlain in 1759. This important battle helped win the war for the British.

In 1759, the British captured Quebec, the capital of New France. The French fought on for another four years, but they were forced to sign a peace treaty in 1763. The English had won. As a result, the French turned over all their territory in North America to the British. New France was renamed Canada.

The war was over but its effects would be felt for years to come. The conflict had cost the British government millions of pounds. These costs would have to be recovered somehow.

War and Profits in New York

Although the war cost the English enormous amounts of money, New York's business owners got rich as it raged on. "War is declared in England—Universal rejoicing among the merchants," one New Yorker wrote in his diary in 1757.

More than 20,000 British troops were sent to America to fight the French and their Indian allies. England stationed most of these army and navy forces in New York City during the war. The city had a large harbor for loading and unloading supply ships and the Hudson River made it easy to move troops closer to New France to fight.

When the colonists first saw the enormous size of the force Britain had sent to America, they were shocked and a little frightened. Then they realized that all these men would need food, clothing, ammunition, entertainment, and shoes—

everything that New York businesses had to offer. The British troops would provide a steady stream of business for years to come.

Profits were also made at sea. **Privateering**, a legal form of piracy, had become big business in New York. Armed with letters saying that they were working for Britain, the captains of privately owned warships set out to capture anything afloat that flew a French flag. Whatever they seized in battle—a

Captain Kidd and Privateering

Born in Scotland, William Kidd was already a successful sea captain when he settled in New York in 1689. There, he started a family and became a wealthy shipowner. He bought property on Wall Street and helped build nearby Trinity Church. Kidd was one of the city's bigwigs.

In 1695, Kidd became a privateer for England. Privateers were the commanders of ships who were paid by countries to attack and capture the ships of their enemies. Kidd set sail in his own ship, the *Adventure Galley*, and began searching the seas for enemies of England. Kidd was supposed to capture only ships from enemy countries. Eventually, however, the temptation of wealth grew so great that Kidd and his crew attacked any ship they could find and took whatever it was carrying. This made Kidd a pirate, not a privateer. When he returned to New York, he was put in irons (handcuffs and leg chains) and sent to London. After a quick trial, he was hanged on May 23, 1701.

ship, its cargo, its passengers' belongings—the privateers could keep. They would then sell what they had taken and divide the profits with the people who had hired them. Many New Yorkers got rich this way.

Rumblings of Revolution

All this moneymaking did not escape the notice of England's King George III and his prime minister, William Pitt. The war against France had cost England a tremendous amount of money. The two men decided to get some of that money back from their colonies in America. Taxing the colonists seemed to be the best way to accomplish this goal, but the taxes would prove to be a huge problem for the people of New York.

When the French and Indian War ended in 1763, New York's economy was crushed. The troops left for home, and so did their money. The New York newspaper *Post Boy* put it simply: "Our business of all kinds is stopped." Many shops and businesses—and the people who worked in them—were no longer needed. Thousands of workers were suddenly unemployed. Shops closed, and many people lost their homes.

The British government did not care about these problems. It wanted the colonists to pay some of the costs of the war. In 1765, Britain's governing body, called Parliament, passed the Stamp Act. The act created a tax on all paper and

The Stamp Act required all paper products sold in the colonies to have stamps like these attached to them.

paper products sold in the colonies. Colonists had to buy stamps (similar to postage stamps) and place them on all legal documents such as wills and marriage certificates, as well as on stationary, playing cards, and newspapers. This was the first direct tax on the colonies by Britain. The Americans were furious.

In New York City, angry mobs destroyed the homes of the governor and his officials. The Stamp Act set off similar riots in the other colonies. As a result, representatives from nine of the thirteen colonies gathered in New York City to decide what to do. The meeting was called the Stamp Act **Congress**. The **delegates** at the congress sent a letter to the British government demanding that it do away with the tax. The British ignored this demand.

New Yorkers decided to resist Britain's demand that they pay the tax. Two hundred merchants agreed to stop buying British goods. A mob of more than 2,000 surrounded the British fort where the stamps were stored. Similar protests

The Sons of Liberty

The Stamp Act Congress was only one way that colonists fought British taxes. Colonial merchants and tradesmen banded together to form a secret society called the Sons of Liberty. This group's main purpose was to attack the British tax collectors with words and violence. They even chased tax collectors with clubs and hung dummies dressed as tax collectors from trees.

The Stamp Act was repealed. However, the Sons of Liberty continued to attack people who supported the British cause. In May 1776, the Sons of Liberty in New York City stopped a theater performance that was attended by **Loyalists**. They made everyone go outside. Then, they destroyed the theater building and started a bonfire with the wood.

These acts helped unite the colonists. They also convinced the British to send more troops to America to stop the protests.

occurred throughout the other colonies. These actions forced the British government to repeal the Stamp Act in 1766.

The Stamp Act Congress was the first time the British colonies united against their rulers. Some colonists had already begun to call themselves Americans instead of Englishmen. Over the next decade, further actions by the British would forge the colonies into a united people.

A Shot Heard 'Round the World

In 1767, George III was still determined to raise money from the colonies. Britain's Parliament passed the Townshend Acts. These new laws broke up the New York Assembly and placed a tax on tea and other imported goods.

Americans loved tea. More than a million of them drank it twice a day. Now they would have to pay more for it and other goods imported from England. Because of their large populations, Boston and New York City were hit especially hard by the Townshend Acts. Once again, people in New York and other colonial cities took to the streets and protested.

A year after the law was passed, British troops were sent to Boston to control the colonists.

For two years, angry mobs came close to fighting with the British troops. Finally, in 1770, the Bostonians rioted, and a few were killed by British soldiers. The incident, known as the Boston Massacre, outraged Americans.

The famous Boston Tea Party came in 1773. Angry **Patriots** calling themselves the Sons of Liberty dressed as Indians to hide their true identities. They boarded a British ship and threw its cargo of tea into Boston's harbor. In New York, a similar group gave the same treatment to a British ship in the harbor. They did not even bother to dress up like Indians during this open act of rebellion.

In 1774, the thirteen colonies sent delegates to a meeting called the Continental Congress in Philadelphia, Pennsylvania. It was the job of this congress to come up with a plan to put a stop to the unfair rule of England.

The delegates called for the colonists to stop buying British goods. This kind of act is known as a boycott. The Continental Congress also told the colonists to arm them-

selves in case of war with Britain. Soon, colonies formed militias that began training for possible war.

Events boiled over in Massachusetts in April 1775. Seven hundred British troops marched from Boston to

Yankee Doodle

Both the British and the colonists claimed "Yankee Doodle" as their song. The British sang their version of "Yankee Doodle" as a way to mock the colonists:

Yankee Doodle came to town,
For to buy a firelock;
We will tar and feather him
And so we will John Hancock.

(CHORUS)
Yankee Doodle, keep it up,
Yankee Doodle Dandy,
Mind the music and the step,
And with the girls be handy.

After the conflict at Lexington and Concord, the minutemen took the song as their own. Folklore says that the colonists sang this verse as they repelled British soldiers:

Father and I went down to camp,
along with Captain Good'in,
And there we see the men
*   and boys*
as thick as hasty puddin'.

Lexington to stop a group of soldiers who were practicing. These soldiers were called minutemen because they could prepare to fight in a minute. The minutemen held their ground. Eight of them were killed before they could retreat.

The British soldiers then marched to the nearby town of Concord. Their goal was to destroy ammunition and other supplies that the colonial militia had safely stored there. Before they could arrive, the minutemen sprang into action.

The Massachusetts militia met the British troops on the Lexington green in 1775. One Patriot shouted, "If they want a war, let it begin here."

More than 300 minutemen crossed a small bridge outside the town. The minutemen fired their muskets from behind trees and rocks. After a fierce firefight, the British fell back to Boston under a hail of Patriot musket balls. The minutemen killed or injured 300 retreating British soldiers.

At Lexington and Concord, Boston's Patriots had fired what the poet William Wadsworth Longfellow called "the shot heard 'round the world." This marked the first time that American soldiers had defied and even killed British troops. There was no turning back now. The colonists were determined to gain their liberty. The Revolutionary War had begun.

CHAPTER SEVEN

The War for Independence

The Patriots Get Organized

As word of the bloodshed at Lexington and Concord echoed through the colonies, 20,000 Patriots grabbed their muskets and marched to Boston. They soon surrounded and outnumbered the British troops in the city. Young American soldiers began to flex their muscles and show their patriotic spirit.

A second Continental Congress was called in Philadelphia in May 1775. The delegates prepared their people for rebellion. They chose forty-three-year-old George Washington to head the Continental army that was quickly forming outside Boston.

In the meantime, a tiny force under the command of Ethan Allen and Benedict Arnold captured a British fort at

Patriot militiamen defended Breed's Hill outside Boston in the first major battle of the Revolutionary War.

Ticonderoga in upstate New York. This fort guarded New York's upstate lakes, but its capture was important for another reason. Fort Ticonderoga was filled with **artillery** and gunpowder, military supplies that the Patriots desperately needed. Arnold saw to it that this military hardware was transported across New York's rugged mountains to Boston. There, colonial forces had the British army trapped in the city.

In June 1775, from a high point called Breed's Hill just outside Boston, the minutemen lobbed cannonballs at British troops in the city. Both sides were trying to capture another point outside the city called Bunker Hill. The British responded quickly, attacking the 1,500 Patriots holding the hill. After three attempts and the loss of over 1,000 British

Bunker Hill Hero

The British charged up Breed's Hill three times. On the final charge, the Patriots were almost out of ammunition. They were preparing to retreat when British major John Pitcairn directed them to admit defeat. The Patriots seemed to have no choice. Then, a freed slave named Peter Salem rushed forth and shot Pitcairn. In the confusion that followed, the Patriot army escaped.

Salem had been a slave whose owner offered him freedom if he fought for the Patriot army. Salem agreed and fought for the Americans throughout the war. Afterwards, he became a basket maker and lived in Massachusetts.

soldiers, the British eventually won the battle. However, the American militiamen had proved that they could fight against the powerful British army.

In the spring of 1776, the Patriots again attacked the British troops occupying Boston. This time, they used the cannons that Arnold had captured from Fort Ticonderoga. The Patriot army drove the British from the city.

By the summer of 1776, most of America's 2.5 million people were convinced that they had to gain their freedom from England. That June, the Continental Congress asked a committee headed by a Virginian named Thomas Jefferson to write a Declaration of Independence. The purpose of this document was to tell King George III once and for all that America was going to be a separate country. Delegates from all of the thirteen colonies voted to approve the Declaration of Independence on July 4, 1776, and on August 2 they met again to sign it. The delegates knew that their lives were now on the line. If the Patriots lost the war, everyone who had signed the Declaration of Independence could be hanged as a traitor.

The War Comes to New York City

When the British abandoned Boston in the spring, they needed a new base of operations from which to fight against the colonists. They chose New York City. In July 1776, as the ink dried on the Declaration of Independence, a huge British fleet of 500 ships carrying 35,000 men arrived off the coast of Long Island. The masts of the fleet looked like "a wood of pine trees," one witness said. "I could not believe my eyes," he added. "I declare that I thought all London was afloat."

General Washington was also on the scene in New York City. He commanded a ragtag, ill-trained force of 18,000. Washington and his commanders struggled to fortify Manhattan against the coming invasion.

Tensions grew in the city through the summer of 1776. Britain's General William Howe and his men were camped on Staten Island in New York Harbor. On August 22, Howe landed 15,000 of his troops in Brooklyn, New York. Local Brooklyn and Staten Island militias were filled with men loyal to England who joined the English forces. As more British troops landed, their number swelled to 21,000.

Washington fought the British on Long Island, but his troops could not hold out against their greater numbers. After several days, he had to retreat into Manhattan in order to save his army from complete destruction. As it turned out, this retreat kept the Revolutionary War alive. If Washington's army had been destroyed on Long Island, the Revolution would have ended in 1776.

When the American troops entered the city, they found it almost deserted. Most of the residents had already fled to the surrounding countryside. Washington set up camp and waited for the British to make their next move.

On October 15, 1776, Howe landed 9,000 British soldiers at Kip's Bay in Manhattan. British warships fired hundreds of cannonballs into the city. The Americans had no choice. They fled north, leaving behind mountains of military supplies. During the retreat, a fire raged through southern Manhattan, gutting Trinity Church and hundreds of homes and businesses. No one seemed to know how it had started. Washington, watching the flames from his temporary headquarters in upper Manhattan, was heard to say, "Providence, or some good honest fellow, has done more for us than we were disposed [prepared] to do ourselves." The fire kept the supplies left by Washington's army out of British hands.

Loyal to Britain

Throughout the Revolutionary War, one-third of all Americans were loyal to the British Crown. They were called Loyalists or Tories. In major cities like New York, Loyalists made up a large part of the population. Patriot groups like the Sons of Liberty bullied the Tories and grabbed their property. Many Tories fled the city and American soldiers quickly took over their houses.

British New York

The British found New York City in ruins. The fire that had devastated the southwest quarter of Manhattan had put many of the city's poor on the street. The British authorities ignored their troubles. The poor citizens could build only a filthy tent village where their homes once stood. Meanwhile, the upper classes, which were mostly Loyalist, rejoiced in the return of royal authority.

As each year of the war passed, conditions grew more desperate for the majority of New Yorkers. There were no jobs in the city, and the British distrusted the city's working

class. They thought that most of New York's poor residents were Patriots who supported the American cause. To make matters worse, the British army forced New Yorkers to feed and shelter English soldiers in their homes.

The price of everyday goods rose to new heights. Food prices soared by 800 percent. Poor New Yorkers starved, barely surviving on beans and rice. At the same time, rich Loyalists continued to live well. They enjoyed themselves by throwing parties, playing golf, and hunting foxes.

When Washington's troops retreated from Long Island to Manhattan across the East River, they found New York City almost deserted.

Good News for Black Americans

New York's black population had reason to celebrate the British **conquest** of New York. Shortly after taking over, the British posted a new law promising freedom to those blacks who joined the British army.

Blacks flocked to New York from all over the Northeast as the British made good on their promise. Soon, Loyalist regiments were formed from ranks of these former slaves and servants. These army units had names like the Ethiopian Regiment, the Royal African Regiment, and the Black Brigade. The British army even held parties at which English officers mingled freely with their black counterparts. This caused outrage among many Patriots who had been the owners of these former slaves.

Upstate Invasion

In early 1777, the British devised a plan to seize New York's Hudson River valley, north of New York City. Sometimes called the Breadbasket of the Revolution, the valley was filled with farms and iron foundries that provided food and weapons for Patriot soldiers and their families. The British wanted to cut off these supplies to the Patriots and take them for themselves.

According to the British plan, General John "Gentleman Johnny" Burgoyne would fight his way southward from Canada, across the chain of upstate lakes, and down the Hudson River. At the same time, a smaller British force would sweep in from Lake Ontario in the west. Finally, General Howe would move north from Manhattan. New York's Patriots would be squeezed between the three armies.

The British army was forced to surrender to the Americans after the Battle of Saratoga.

General Burgoyne's plan required him to command an army of 8,000 men. This force would head down the length of Lake Champlain on simple, flat-decked wooden boats. When it got to the Hudson River, it would attack the Americans in the valley, driving them out.

A Soldier's Life

The life of the American soldiers fighting in northern New York was always dirty, often boring, and occasionally deadly. In the Continental army or the militias, the daily routine was the same—like camping in bad weather without enough equipment.

Soldiers in the Continental army often had ragged clothes and poor equipment.

The moment a man signed up for his six-month hitch in the colonial army, he was entitled to five dollars a month. If he brought his own gun, he was paid a little more. The soldier was also promised new clothes, bedding, and cooking supplies, but generally, the Continental Congress did not have enough money to provide them.

What kept most Continental soldiers fighting was a promise that the congress did keep. Every man who did his six months' duty was given free land after the war.

98

The Battle of Saratoga

On a bright June morning in 1777, Burgoyne's soldiers climbed onto their flatboats for the trip down Lake Champlain. Bands played and the sun shone. At first, the plan went perfectly. Fort Ticonderoga fell to the British almost without a fight. Burgoyne chased the fleeing Americans down the lake.

What Burgoyne did not know was that his entire army was heading into a trap. For his plan to work, he needed the farmers of upstate New York to join his side. They would have to provide food and transportation for his men. However, among Burgoyne's troops were a number of Huron Indians. The Huron hated the white settlers who had stolen their land, and the New York farmers hated and feared the Indians.

Most of the farmers did not care about the Revolutionary War. They trusted neither the powerful British nor the Patriots in the big city. When Burgoyne announced that any New Yorkers who failed to join with the British would have their farms burned by Indians, the settlers then knew which side they were on. Almost to a man, the farmers decided to take up arms and "go agin' [against] Burgoyne."

Burgoyne's army had to hack a path and build a road through the forest. As the British soldiers headed down this road, American soldiers and angry farmers fired on the column from all directions. Burgoyne expected General Howe to come up the Hudson to his aid, but Howe never arrived. In early October 1777, American forces attacked and defeated Burgoyne's army. On October 17, the British surrendered at the town of Saratoga. The whole series of skirmishes, raids, and ambushes that made up this fight would be known as the Battle of Saratoga.

New Hope From Saratoga

When the Battle of Saratoga ended, General Washington was bottled up at Valley Forge, Pennsylvania. His troops had spent a bitterly cold, harsh winter just trying to survive. Food, blankets, and other supplies were scarce. Some Continental soldiers were now fighting without shoes, tramping through the biting snow barefoot. While England had the largest army in the world, the colonies had only the small numbers of troops that the Continental Congress had raised. Soon, many of these soldiers' six-month contracts would be up. It would be hard to convince the soldiers to continue the fight for freedom without some hopeful sign that they had a chance of winning the war. The victory at Saratoga in the northern woods of New York provided that hope.

The Continental army led by George Washington spent the long cold winter of 1777–1778 encamped at Valley Forge, Pennsylvania.

Since the fighting began at Lexington in 1775, France had secretly been providing about 90 percent of the Patriots' gunpowder, as well as other weapons. The French were still bitter over their defeat in the French and Indian War. They had agreed to help the Americans fight the British as a way of getting back at their old enemy.

The triumph at Saratoga made it clear that the colonies had the spirit to fight and win. The French were ready to sign a formal treaty to give them aid. From 1778 on, France joined forces with America to fight their common enemy, England. The French made their support of the Americans clear and visible by sending a fleet of warships to Rhode Island.

The War Ends

Even after the victory at Saratoga, the Patriot army had a difficult time against the more powerful British forces. In 1781, the Patriot cause entered its darkest hours. The American army was threatening mutiny over lack of back pay. In addition, all the colonies were running out of money because of the huge costs of the war. Squabbling between the colonies over money was getting worse. It was just at that moment that a blundering British general named Charles Cornwallis stumbled into a trap, bringing the war to a successful end for the Americans.

Cornwallis commanded an army of 7,000 British troops. After a failed campaign in North and South Carolina, he and his army fell back to the port of Yorktown, Virginia. He hoped to get resupplied by the British navy there. However, the French fleet had beaten British ships in a huge naval battle in nearby Chesapeake Bay. Instead of the British fleet waiting with supplies, Cornwallis met French ships and their cannons at Yorktown.

When General Washington got word of the French naval victory, he swiftly marched his 8,000 troops 300 miles (480 kilometers) from New York City to Yorktown. Joining him were another 8,000 French soldiers. Without supplies or fresh soldiers, Cornwallis surrendered his forces on October 17, 1781, after a few short weeks of fighting. As his 7,000 men marched out to surrender, their bands played the popular tune "The World Turn'd Upside Down."

For the British, the world had indeed been turned upside down. The powerful British army had been defeated by a band of farmers and tradesmen.

CHAPTER EIGHT

Statehood for New York

Peace in Paris, Problems at Home

The treaty that ended the war was worked out and signed in Paris, the capital of France, in the summer of 1783. For most New Yorkers, however, the true end of the Revolutionary War came with the arrival of General Washington and his troops in New York City on November 25, 1783. Known as Evacuation Day, this was the day the British troops left New York and the United States.

The defeated British soldiers marched down the broad avenue of the Bowery and climbed into boats on the East River. Marching behind them, with enough of a gap to prevent trouble, were the soldiers of the Continental army. Someone who was there recalled,

General George Washington said good-bye to his troops at Fraunces's Tavern in New York City in 1783.

The troops just leaving were as if equipped for show...and with their scarlet uniforms and burnished arms, made a brilliant display. The troops that marched in, however, were ill-clad and weather-beaten, and made a forlorn appearance. But then they were our troops, and as I looked at them, and thought upon all they had done for us, my heart and my eyes were full, and I admired and gloried in them the more because they were weather-beaten and forlorn.

Along with the British troops, thousands of Loyalists boarded ships for England and Canada. Washington demanded that the British return any escaped slaves who were living in New York. The British refused, and more than 4,000 black Americans left the United States for good.

Washington and his officers met a few days later at Fraunces's Tavern, which had been the scene of many revolutionary meetings. As his fellow soldiers embraced the general for the last time as their military commander, fireworks went off throughout the city. The officers and their troops drank many toasts.

A New Government

The thirteen colonies were now the United States of America. The war was over, but the new country faced big problems. Differences between small and large states threatened to tear the new nation apart.

The northern states had more large towns and cities than the South. The North relied mostly on shipping, fishing, and trade by sea; small farms dotted its inland territory. The southern states had few cities but many large farms, called plantations, owned by a powerful upper class of farmers. The southern states depended on slaves to work the plantations.

The national government that was supposed to unite all these states had almost no power. A document called the Articles of Confederation had held the states loosely together during the Revolutionary War. But it was clear that the Articles of Confederation would not be enough to govern the new nation.

The First Capital

New York City became the capital of the United States in 1785 after the Revolutionary War. In 1790, the capital was moved to Philadelphia and then, in 1800, to Washington, D.C.

The new United States also faced financial problems. The government could not pay its debts to countries such as France, who had helped during the war. In addition, with only 700 men now in its national army, the United States could not defend itself from foreign attack. Americans feared most the very real possibility of another British invasion. Solutions for all these problems had to be found quickly.

The Constitutional Convention

In the spring of 1787, a convention to strengthen the Articles of Confederation was called in Philadelphia. New York sent three delegates, including a brilliant lawyer named Alexander Hamilton. Hamilton and others argued that a whole new set of laws was needed.

In a five-hour speech, Hamilton argued for a stronger federal (central) government. Such a government would give the country the respect and power it would need to conduct trade with other nations and protect its people at home. Most of the fifty-five delegates at the convention agreed with Hamilton, but it would take several **compromises** and a long hot summer of argument before all the delegates agreed.

For months, the delegates worked to write a new set of laws to govern the country. The document they created is called the **Constitution** of the United States of America.

Women and the Vote

The new freedoms offered to American citizens by the Constitution did not apply to everyone. Slaves had almost no rights and were excluded from voting. In addition, women could not vote in the new United States.

During colonial times, women did not take an active role in politics. Most people believed that women should concern themselves only with raising their families. At the time, women under the age of twenty-one were under the legal control of their fathers. Once married, they came under the legal control of their husbands. Women could not own property or make legal decisions for themselves. Because they had few legal rights, women did not participate in politics.

During the Revolution, some women started to express their political beliefs in private

Abigail Adams was married to John Adams, the second president of the United States. She spoke out for more rights for women in the young United States.

conversations and in letters. Women like Abigail Adams sought greater legal rights for women. But this had very little effect on the U.S. Constitution or the individual state constitutions. Women were not given the right to vote in the United States until the Nineteenth Amendment to the Constitution was passed in 1920.

The Great Compromise

The Constitution resulted from a great compromise that allowed both small and large states to have an equal say in the **federal government**. The Constitution created the Congress, the court system, and the executive branch of government headed by the president. All other laws in the nation, including state laws, must agree with the Constitution.

On September 17, 1787, the delegates signed the Constitution. This document would become the supreme law of the land. But first the delegates had to carry the Constitution back to their own states for approval. As each state approved the document, it would officially join the United States. When a two-thirds majority, or nine states, agreed to the new laws, the Constitution would become legally binding for those states.

New York's representatives were in no hurry to sign the new Constitution. Because New York was the most powerful of the colonies, its leaders felt that it stood to lose the most by banding together with its smaller, weaker neighbors. Also, many New Yorkers resented outside authority and disliked the idea of a powerful central government. For almost a year, New Yorkers argued over the issue of statehood, writing pamphlets, newspapers, and essays called broadsides to present their views.

George Washington arrived in New York City aboard a barge rowed by thirteen oarsmen. He was met by cheering crowds, bands, and fireworks displays.

Eventually, another compromise settled the matter. A Bill of Rights would be added to the Constitution. The Bill of Rights contained the first ten amendments (additions) to the Constitution. These amendments guaranteed the citizens' individual liberties that many New Yorkers had feared would be taken away by a strong national government. On July 26, 1788, New York became the eleventh state to sign the Constitution.

A Presidential "Coronation" in New York City

On April 30, 1789, New York City threw one of the biggest parties in its history. George Washington was coming to town to be inaugurated as the first president of the United States. Washington wanted "a quiet entry into the city, devoid of ceremony," but the people had other ideas. There had never been a presidential inauguration before, so people treated this one as though they were crowning a king.

As Washington neared Manhattan, church bells rang out. Cannons boomed. Roses were thrown at his feet. Thirteen boat pilots (one for each state) steered his ceremonial barge across the Hudson River. When the barge landed, a purple carpet was laid at his feet. Then the man who was already being called "the father of our country" walked to Federal Hall. People jammed the narrow lanes around Wall Street to see his swearing-in.

As the president took the oath of office, "the scene was solemn and awful [full of awe] beyond description," one spectator wrote. Then, with a booming voice, Robert Livingston, the Chancellor of New York State, who had given the oath, bellowed, "Long live George Washington, the President of the United States!" The crowd repeated the cry over and over.

George Washington was sworn in as the first president of the United States on the balcony of Federal Hall in New York City.

The party that followed continued long into the night. Huge bonfires illuminated paintings showing heroic scenes from the Revolutionary War. A two-hour fireworks display boomed overhead, and all the ships in the harbor lit torches. The streets were so crowded that President Washington, who celebrated his inauguration at Livingston's house, had to make his way home on foot because there was no room in the streets for a carriage or horse.

A State Comes of Age

This new country, the United States, was something unique in the world. It was a nation forged from the shared values of its citizens. New York and its people played a central role in the struggle that formed the nation. In a sense, the story of New York's birth and growth is the story of the entire United States. From the Dutch colonists' first demands for individual rights and self-government to the Patriots' decision to fight British tyranny, New York showed the character for which all Americans would soon be known.

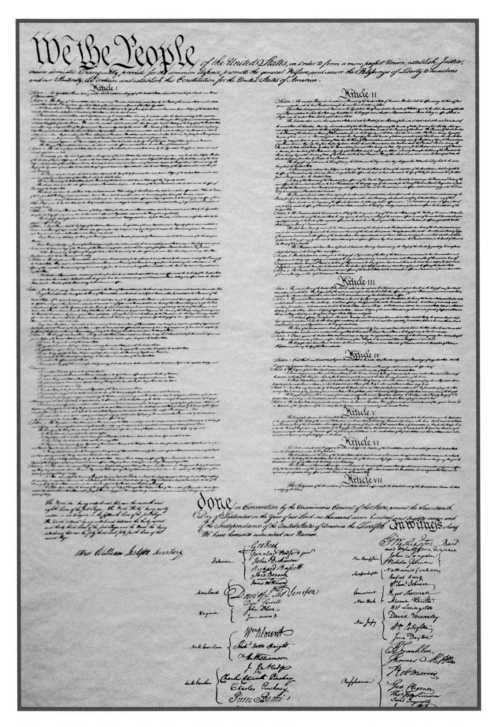

The original Constitution of the United States was written by hand. However, copies were soon published in every newspaper in the country.

115

Recipe
Apple Butter

Colonial families loved apples. They could be stored for long periods and used in a large number of colonial dishes. One of these was apple butter. This sweet colonial favorite could be spread on bread to make a tasty treat.

9 pounds ripe apples
3 1/2 quarts apple cider
1 1/2 cups packed brown sugar
1 cup of molasses
2 teaspoons ground cloves
2 teaspoons cinnamon
1 teaspoon allspice
1/2 teaspoon salt
Sassafras bark (optional)

- Peel, core, and quarter apples.

- Cook cider over high heat in an uncovered pot until half the liquid is gone.

- Add apples to the hot cider.

- Lower heat and cook apples in cider until soft.

- Press cider and apple chunks through a food mill until pureed.

- Return puree to the pot.

- Add sugar, molasses, spices, and salt.

- Cook puree over low heat, stirring until the apple mixture thickens into butter.

- Pour apple butter into containers.

- Optional: Place a small piece of sassafras bark in each container for added spice.

- Place lid on container and cool.

This activity should be done with adult supervision.

Activity
Tinware

Decorating boxes and other items made from tin dates back to colonial times. This metal was soft and easy to mold into interesting and useful shapes. To decorate their work, crafts-people made patterns in the tin by poking holes or cutting slits into it. This produced beautiful household objects, including boxes to hold important papers, and food strainers.

Try making these decorative tinware tiles.

Directions

lightweight tin, found in craft stores
paper • pen or pencil • masking tape
heavyweight cardboard

Note: *aluminum foil may be substituted for the tin.*

- Cut the tin, paper, and cardboard into 4-inch squares.
- Draw or trace the outline of a familiar object on the square of paper.
- Make a sandwich by placing the cardboard on the bottom, the tin in the middle, and the paper on the top.
- Tape the tin sandwich together around the edges.
- Using the pen or pencil, create an imprint around the outline of your drawing by punching a series of holes. Or trace the outline, pressing hard to make a groove in the tin.
- Remove the tape and take the sandwich apart.
- Notice the "tin punch" or depression in the tin in the shape of the object you drew.
- Repeat process to create several decorative tiles.
- Frame them as a group or singly.

This activity should be done with adult supervision.

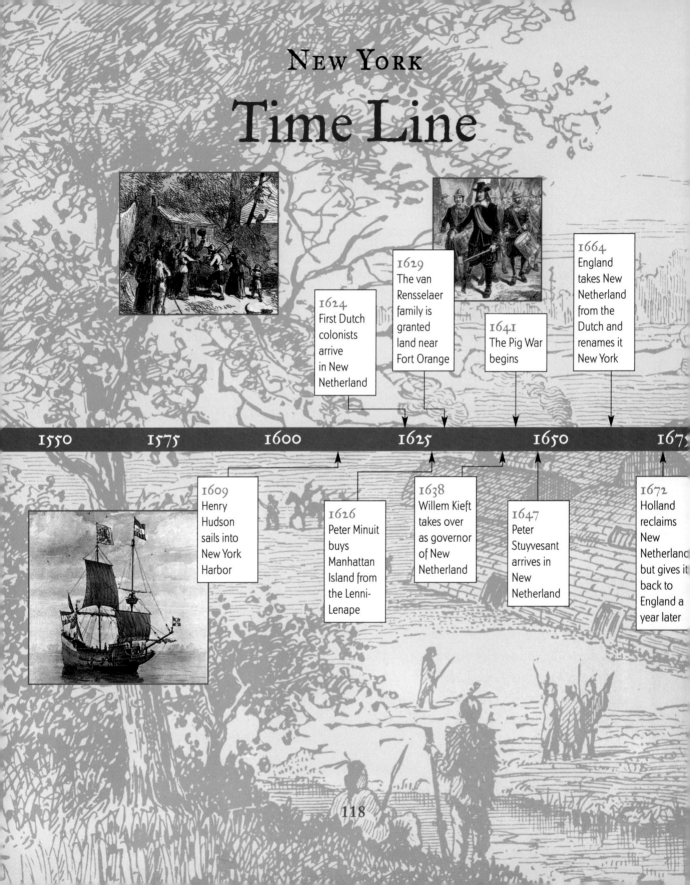

NEW YORK
Time Line

1624
First Dutch colonists arrive in New Netherland

1629
The van Rensselaer family is granted land near Fort Orange

1641
The Pig War begins

1664
England takes New Netherland from the Dutch and renames it New York

1550   1575   1600   1625   1650   1675

1609
Henry Hudson sails into New York Harbor

1626
Peter Minuit buys Manhattan Island from the Lenni-Lenape

1638
Willem Kieft takes over as governor of New Netherland

1647
Peter Stuyvesant arrives in New Netherland

1672
Holland reclaims New Netherland but gives it back to England a year later

118

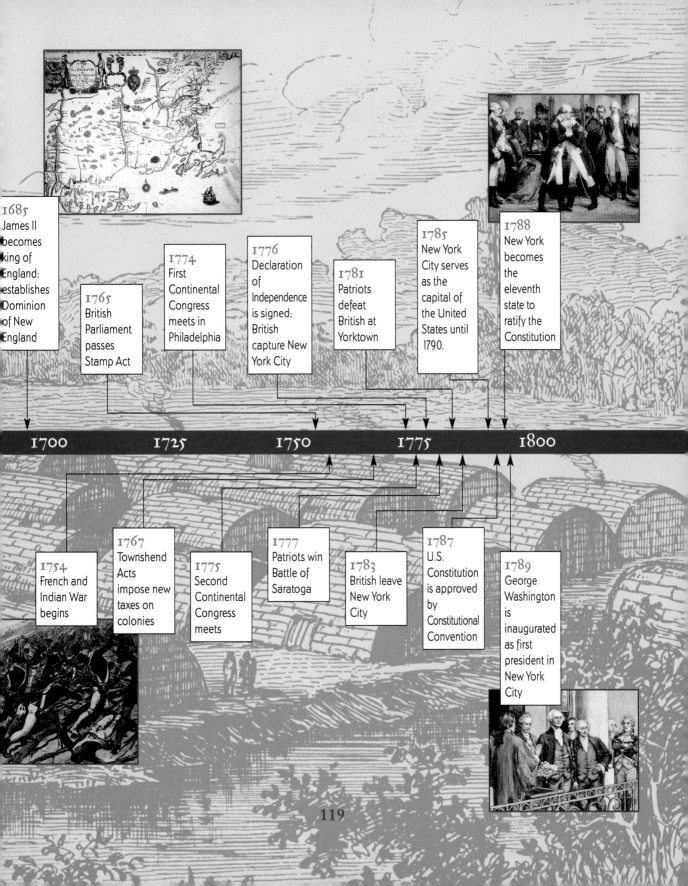

1685
James II becomes king of England; establishes Dominion of New England

1765
British Parliament passes Stamp Act

1774
First Continental Congress meets in Philadelphia

1776
Declaration of Independence is signed; British capture New York City

1781
Patriots defeat British at Yorktown

1785
New York City serves as the capital of the United States until 1790.

1788
New York becomes the eleventh state to ratify the Constitution

1700   1725   1750   1775   1800

1754
French and Indian War begins

1767
Townshend Acts impose new taxes on colonies

1775
Second Continental Congress meets

1777
Patriots win Battle of Saratoga

1783
British leave New York City

1787
U.S. Constitution is approved by Constitutional Convention

1789
George Washington is inaugurated as first president in New York City

119

Further Reading

Gray, Edward G. *Colonial America: A History in Documents.* New York: Oxford University Press, 2003.

Hawke, David Freeman. *Everyday Life in Early America.* New York: Harper and Row, 1988.

Kalman, Bobbie. *Colonial Crafts.* New York: Crabtree Publishers, 1992.

Penner, Lucile Richt. *The Colonial Cookbook.* New York: Hastings House, 1976.

Purvis, Thomas L. *Almanacs of American Life: Colonial America to 1763.* New York: Facts On File, 1999.

Taylor, Dale. *The Writer's Guide to Everyday Life in Colonial America.* Cincinnati, OH: Writer's Digest Books, 1997.

Glossary

alliance an agreement to work together toward a common goal

artillery powerful guns attached to wheels or tracks

blacksmith a person who makes horseshoes and tools from heated iron

cobblestone a flat rock that was used to pave roads in colonial times

colonist person who moves to a distant place but continues to be a citizen of his or her homeland

compromise agreement reached by two sides in which each side gives up some of its demands

congress an official gathering of lawmakers or delegates

conquest defeating an enemy in war

constitution a country, state, or organization's basic system of laws that describes the powers of government and the rights of the citizens

delegate a person who is selected to act or speak for others at a meeting

federal government the union of many states under one central authority

impose to inflict something that is not wanted on another

Loyalist during the American Revolution, someone who was loyal to the British cause, sometimes called a Tory

militia ordinary citizens trained in the military but only called upon in time of war or threat

pamphlet a small booklet with information on a single topic

Patriot in the American Revolution, someone who sided with the colonists fighting the British

privateer the captain of a privately owned ship authorized by a government during wartime to attack and capture enemy vessels

repeal to undo, cancel, or abolish a law

sawmill a large building where logs are sawed into wood

stockade strong posts attached to each other and set upright in the ground to form a barrier

trapper a person who sets traps to capture animals for their fur

Index